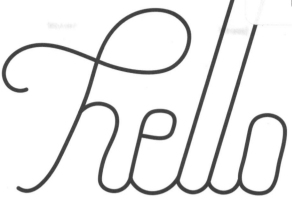

Hello

_____

THIS PLANNER BELONGS TO

_____

SCHOOL

_____

GRADE & ROOM

_____

EMAIL

_____

_____

ADDRESS

_____

PHONE

PLAN ON A

BRILLIANT

Year

NOT TOMORROW — NOT NEXT WEEK

Contacts & VOLUNTEERS

SCHEDULE

SCHOOL BEGINS: _____

LUNCH: _____

RECESS: _____

SPECIALS:

_____

_____

SCHOOL ENDS: _____

NEED HELP?

RELIABLE STUDENTS: _____

_____

TEACHERS: _____

PRINCIPAL: _____

VICE PRINCIPAL: _____

OTHER STAFF: _____

_____

SPECIAL SCHEDULES

NAME	TIME & LOCATION
_____	_____
_____	_____
_____	_____
_____	_____

ADDITIONAL NOTES

_____

_____

_____

_____

_____

COMMUNICATION Log

DATE	TYPE	NAME	PURPOSE	NOTES
	🔲 @ 📋 👥			
	🔲 @ 📋 👥			
	🔲 @ 📋 👥			
	🔲 @ 📋 👥			
	🔲 @ 📋 👥			
	🔲 @ 📋 👥			
	🔲 @ 📋 👥			
	🔲 @ 📋 👥			
	🔲 @ 📋 👥			
	🔲 @ 📋 👥			
	🔲 @ 📋 👥			
	🔲 @ 📋 👥			
	🔲 @ 📋 👥			
	🔲 @ 📋 👥			
	🔲 @ 📋 👥			
	🔲 @ 📋 👥			
	🔲 @ 📋 👥			
	🔲 @ 📋 👥			
	🔲 @ 📋 👥			
	🔲 @ 📋 👥			
	🔲 @ 📋 👥			
	🔲 @ 📋 👥			
	🔲 @ 📋 👥			
	🔲 @ 📋 👥			
	🔲 @ 📋 👥			
	🔲 @ 📋 👥			

COMMUNICATION *Log*

DATE	TYPE	NAME	PURPOSE	NOTES
	▢ @ ▤ 👥			
	▢ @ ▤ 👥			
	▢ @ ▤ 👥			
	▢ @ ▤ 👥			
	▢ @ ▤ 👥			
	▢ @ ▤ 👥			
	▢ @ ▤ 👥			
	▢ @ ▤ 👥			
	▢ @ ▤ 👥			
	▢ @ ▤ 👥			
	▢ @ ▤ 👥			
	▢ @ ▤ 👥			
	▢ @ ▤ 👥			
	▢ @ ▤ 👥			
	▢ @ ▤ 👥			
	▢ @ ▤ 👥			
	▢ @ ▤ 👥			
	▢ @ ▤ 👥			
	▢ @ ▤ 👥			
	▢ @ ▤ 👥			
	▢ @ ▤ 👥			
	▢ @ ▤ 👥			
	▢ @ ▤ 👥			
	▢ @ ▤ 👥			
	▢ @ ▤ 👥			
	▢ @ ▤ 👥			
	▢ @ ▤ 👥			

News AND NOTES

News AND NOTES

 Plan IT

Use these pages to create a classroom plan, record seating charts, create checklists, sketch plans, etc. The options are endless!

Year at a Glance

JULY

AUGUST

SEPTEMBER

OCTOBER

NOVEMBER

DECEMBER

Year at a Glance

JANUARY

FEBRUARY

MARCH

APRIL

MAY

JUNE

Sunday	Monday	Tuesday	Wednesday

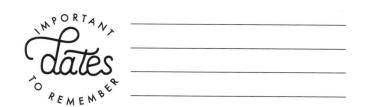

IMPORTANT
Dates
TO REMEMBER

_____
_____
_____

Goals _____
_____
_____

Thursday	Friday	Saturday	To Do
			☐ _____
			☐ _____
			☐ _____
			☐ _____
			☐ _____
			☐ _____
			☐ _____
			☐ _____
			☐ _____
			☐ _____
			☐ _____
			Notes
			_____
			_____
			_____
			_____
			_____
			_____
			_____
			_____

PSST! USE THESE GUIDES TO KEEP YOUR TABS PERFECTLY PLACED.

YOUR ONLY
LIMIT
IS you.

Sunday	Monday	Tuesday	Wednesday

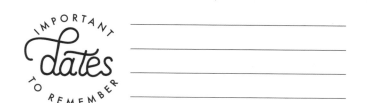

Goals

Thursday	Friday	Saturday	To Do
			☐ _____
			☐ _____
			☐ _____
			☐ _____
			☐ _____
			☐ _____
			☐ _____
			☐ _____
			☐ _____
			☐ _____
			☐ _____
			☐ _____

Notes

September

DON'T STOP
UNTIL
YOU'RE
Proud.

Sunday	Monday	Tuesday	Wednesday

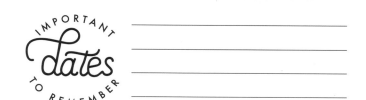
Goals _____

Thursday	Friday	Saturday	To Do
			☐ _____
			☐ _____
			☐ _____
			☐ _____
			☐ _____
			☐ _____
			☐ _____
			☐ _____
			☐ _____
			☐ _____
			☐ _____

Notes

15

September

DON'T STOP
UNTIL
YOU'RE
Proud.

Sunday	Monday	Tuesday	Wednesday

Goals

Thursday	Friday	Saturday	To Do
			☐ _____
			☐ _____
			☐ _____
			☐ _____
			☐ _____
			☐ _____
			☐ _____
			☐ _____
			☐ _____
			☐ _____
			☐ _____
			Notes
			_____
			_____
			_____
			_____
			_____

October

YOU ARE *unstoppable.*

Sunday	Monday	Tuesday	Wednesday

Goals
_____
_____
_____

Thursday	Friday	Saturday	To Do
			☐ _____
			☐ _____
			☐ _____
			☐ _____
			☐ _____
			☐ _____
			☐ _____
			☐ _____
			☐ _____
			☐ _____
			☐ _____
			☐ _____

Notes

November

MAKE TODAY count.

Sunday	Monday	Tuesday	Wednesday

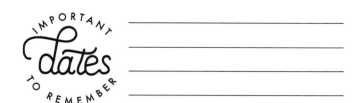
Goals

Thursday	Friday	Saturday	To Do
			☐ _____
			☐ _____
			☐ _____
			☐ _____
			☐ _____
			☐ _____
			☐ _____
			☐ _____
			☐ _____
			☐ _____
			☐ _____

Notes

December

THINK positive, be POSITIVE.

Sunday	Monday	Tuesday	Wednesday

Thursday	Friday	Saturday	To Do
			☐ _____
			☐ _____
			☐ _____
			Notes

January

BE PRESENT.

Sunday	Monday	Tuesday	Wednesday

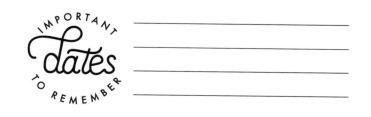

IMPORTANT
Dates
TO REMEMBER

Goals

Thursday	Friday	Saturday

To Do

- ☐ _____
- ☐ _____
- ☐ _____
- ☐ _____
- ☐ _____
- ☐ _____
- ☐ _____
- ☐ _____
- ☐ _____
- ☐ _____
- ☐ _____
- ☐ _____
- ☐ _____

Notes

Sunday	Monday	Tuesday	Wednesday

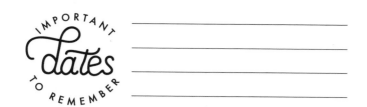

Goals

Thursday	Friday	Saturday	To Do
			☐ _____
			☐ _____
			☐ _____
			☐ _____
			☐ _____
			☐ _____
			☐ _____
			☐ _____
			☐ _____
			☐ _____
			☐ _____
			☐ _____
			Notes

 March

LIFE IS beauty-FULL.

Sunday	Monday	Tuesday	Wednesday

Thursday	Friday	Saturday	To Do
			☐ _____
			☐ _____
			☐ _____
			☐ _____
			☐ _____
			☐ _____
			☐ _____
			☐ _____
			☐ _____
			☐ _____
			☐ _____
			☐ _____
			Notes
			_____
			_____
			_____
			_____
			_____
			_____

April

Sunday	Monday	Tuesday	Wednesday

Thursday	Friday	Saturday	To Do
			☐ _____
			☐ _____
			☐ _____
			☐ _____
			☐ _____
			☐ _____
			☐ _____
			☐ _____
			☐ _____
			☐ _____
			☐ _____
			☐ _____
			Notes

May

Progress IS Progress,
NO MATTER HOW SLOW.

Sunday	Monday	Tuesday	Wednesday

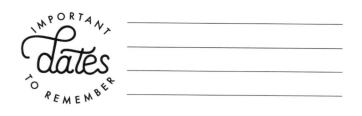

IMPORTANT **dates** TO REMEBER

_____
_____
_____

Goals _____
_____
_____

Thursday	Friday	Saturday	To Do
			☐ _____
			☐ _____
			☐ _____
			☐ _____
			☐ _____
			☐ _____
			☐ _____
			☐ _____
			☐ _____
			☐ _____
			☐ _____
			☐ _____
			☐ _____
			Notes

June

Believe you can,

YOU ARE HALFWAY THERE.

Sunday	Monday	Tuesday	Wednesday

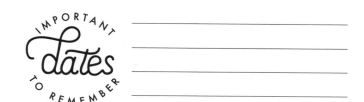

Goals

Thursday	Friday	Saturday	To Do
			☐ ___
			☐ ___
			☐ ___
			☐ ___
			☐ ___
			☐ ___
			☐ ___
			☐ ___
			☐ ___
			☐ ___
			☐ ___
			Notes

Week

SUBJECT	SUBJECT	SUBJECT

Monday /

Tuesday /

Wednesday /

Thursday /

Friday /

SUBJECT	SUBJECT	SUBJECT

SUBJECT	SUBJECT	SUBJECT	SUBJECT

PSST! CUT THIS CORNER OFF EACH WEEK TO MARK AND FIND YOUR PLACE EASILY!

Week

	SUBJECT	SUBJECT	SUBJECT
Monday /			
Tuesday /			
Wednesday /			
Thursday /			
Friday /			

SUBJECT	SUBJECT	SUBJECT	SUBJECT

Week

SUBJECT	SUBJECT	SUBJECT
Monday /			
Tuesday /			
Wednesday /			
Thursday /			
Friday /			

SUBJECT	SUBJECT	SUBJECT

SUBJECT	SUBJECT	SUBJECT	SUBJECT
SUBJECT	SUBJECT	SUBJECT	SUBJECT

Week

	SUBJECT	SUBJECT	SUBJECT
Monday /			
Tuesday /			
Wednesday /			
Thursday /			
Friday /			

SUBJECT	SUBJECT	SUBJECT	SUBJECT

Week

	SUBJECT	SUBJECT	SUBJECT
Monday /			
Tuesday /			
Wednesday /			
Thursday /			
Friday /			

SUBJECT	SUBJECT	SUBJECT	SUBJECT

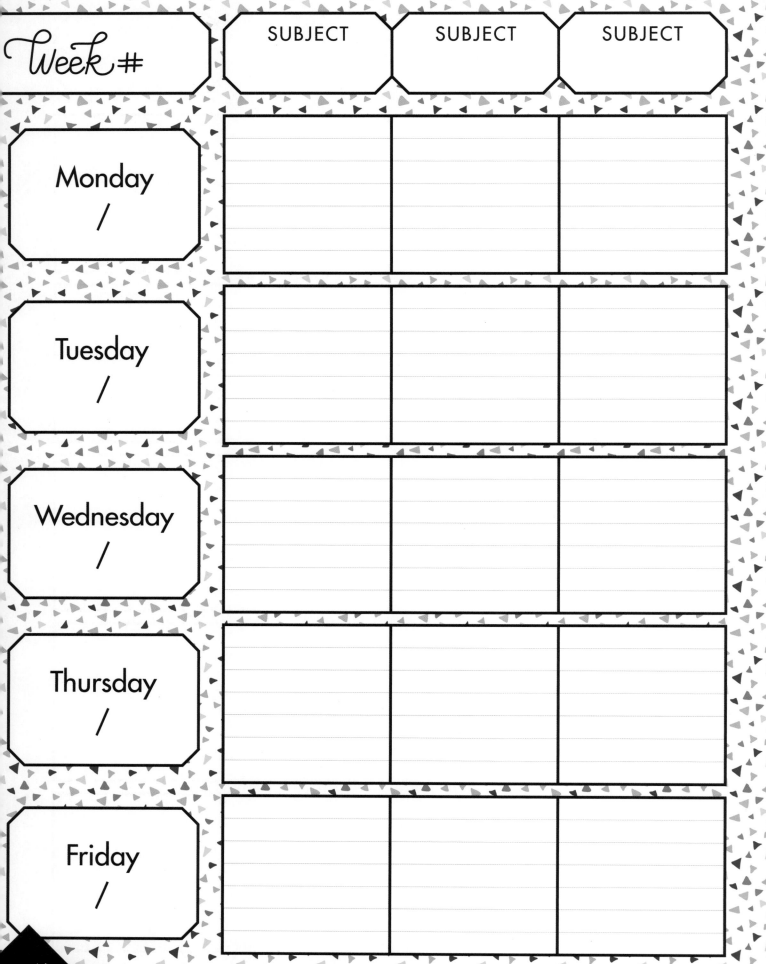

Week #

SUBJECT	SUBJECT	SUBJECT

Monday /

Tuesday /

Wednesday /

Thursday /

Friday /

SUBJECT	SUBJECT	SUBJECT	SUBJECT

Week #	SUBJECT	SUBJECT	SUBJECT
Monday /			
Tuesday /			
Wednesday /			
Thursday /			
Friday /			
	SUBJECT	SUBJECT	SUBJECT

SUBJECT	SUBJECT	SUBJECT	SUBJECT

Week #

SUBJECT	SUBJECT	SUBJECT
Monday /		
Tuesday /		
Wednesday /		
Thursday /		
Friday /		

50

SUBJECT	SUBJECT	SUBJECT	SUBJECT

SUBJECT	SUBJECT	SUBJECT	SUBJECT

	SUBJECT	SUBJECT	SUBJECT
Week #			
Monday /			
Tuesday /			
Wednesday /			
Thursday /			
Friday /			

SUBJECT	SUBJECT	SUBJECT	SUBJECT

Week #

SUBJECT	SUBJECT	SUBJECT

Monday
/

Tuesday
/

Wednesday
/

Thursday
/

Friday
/

SUBJECT	SUBJECT	SUBJECT

SUBJECT	SUBJECT	SUBJECT	SUBJECT

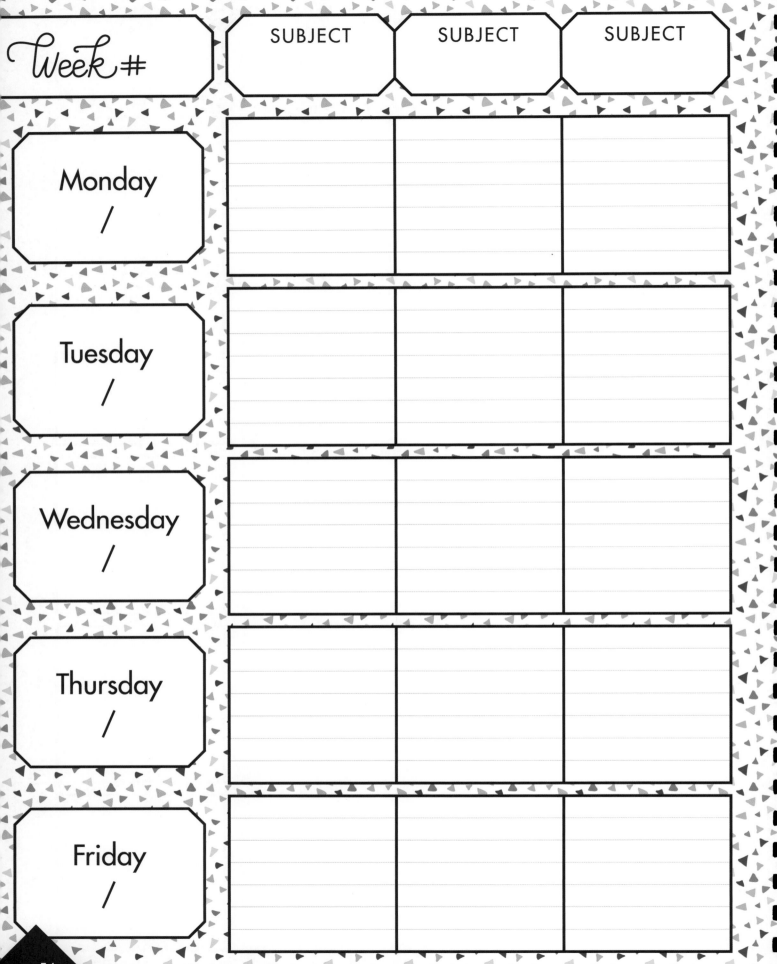

Week #

SUBJECT	SUBJECT	SUBJECT

Monday /

Tuesday /

Wednesday /

Thursday /

Friday /

SUBJECT	SUBJECT	SUBJECT

SUBJECT	SUBJECT	SUBJECT	SUBJECT
SUBJECT	SUBJECT	SUBJECT	SUBJECT

Week

	SUBJECT	SUBJECT	SUBJECT
Monday /			
Tuesday /			
Wednesday /			
Thursday /			
Friday /			

SUBJECT	SUBJECT	SUBJECT	SUBJECT

Week

	SUBJECT	SUBJECT	SUBJECT
Monday /			
Tuesday /			
Wednesday /			
Thursday /			
Friday /			

SUBJECT	SUBJECT	SUBJECT	SUBJECT

Week

	SUBJECT	SUBJECT	SUBJECT
Monday /			
Tuesday /			
Wednesday /			
Thursday /			
Friday /			

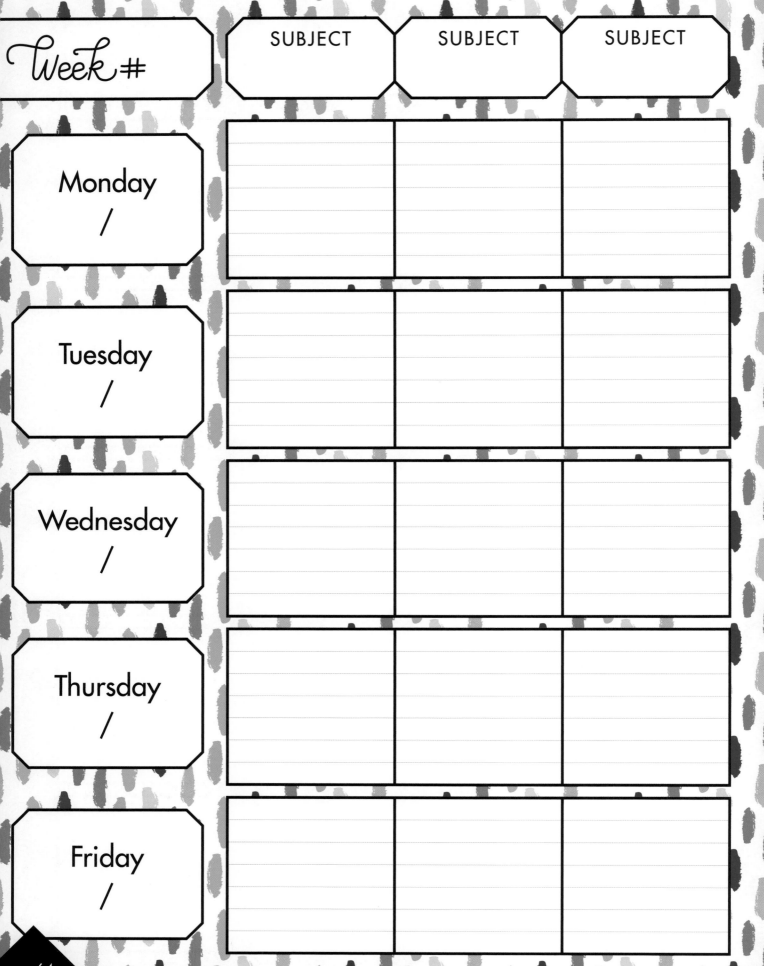

Week #

	SUBJECT	SUBJECT	SUBJECT
Monday /			
Tuesday /			
Wednesday /			
Thursday /			
Friday /			

SUBJECT	SUBJECT	SUBJECT	SUBJECT

Week

	SUBJECT	SUBJECT	SUBJECT
Monday /			
Tuesday /			
Wednesday /			
Thursday /			
Friday /			

SUBJECT	SUBJECT	SUBJECT	SUBJECT

Week

	SUBJECT	SUBJECT	SUBJECT
Monday /			
Tuesday /			
Wednesday /			
Thursday /			
Friday /			

| | SUBJECT | SUBJECT | SUBJECT |

SUBJECT	SUBJECT	SUBJECT	SUBJECT

Week

SUBJECT	SUBJECT	SUBJECT

Monday
/

Tuesday
/

Wednesday
/

Thursday
/

Friday
/

Week

SUBJECT	SUBJECT	SUBJECT

Monday /

Tuesday /

Wednesday /

Thursday /

Friday /

SUBJECT	SUBJECT	SUBJECT

SUBJECT	SUBJECT	SUBJECT	SUBJECT

Week #

SUBJECT	SUBJECT	SUBJECT
Monday /		
Tuesday /		
Wednesday /		
Thursday /		
Friday /		

SUBJECT	SUBJECT	SUBJECT	SUBJECT

Week #

SUBJECT	SUBJECT	SUBJECT

Monday /

Tuesday /

Wednesday /

Thursday /

Friday /

SUBJECT	SUBJECT	SUBJECT	SUBJECT

Week #

SUBJECT	SUBJECT	SUBJECT

Monday
/

Tuesday
/

Wednesday
/

Thursday
/

Friday
/

SUBJECT	SUBJECT	SUBJECT	SUBJECT

	SUBJECT	SUBJECT	SUBJECT
Monday /			
Tuesday /			
Wednesday /			
Thursday /			
Friday /			

SUBJECT	SUBJECT	SUBJECT	SUBJECT

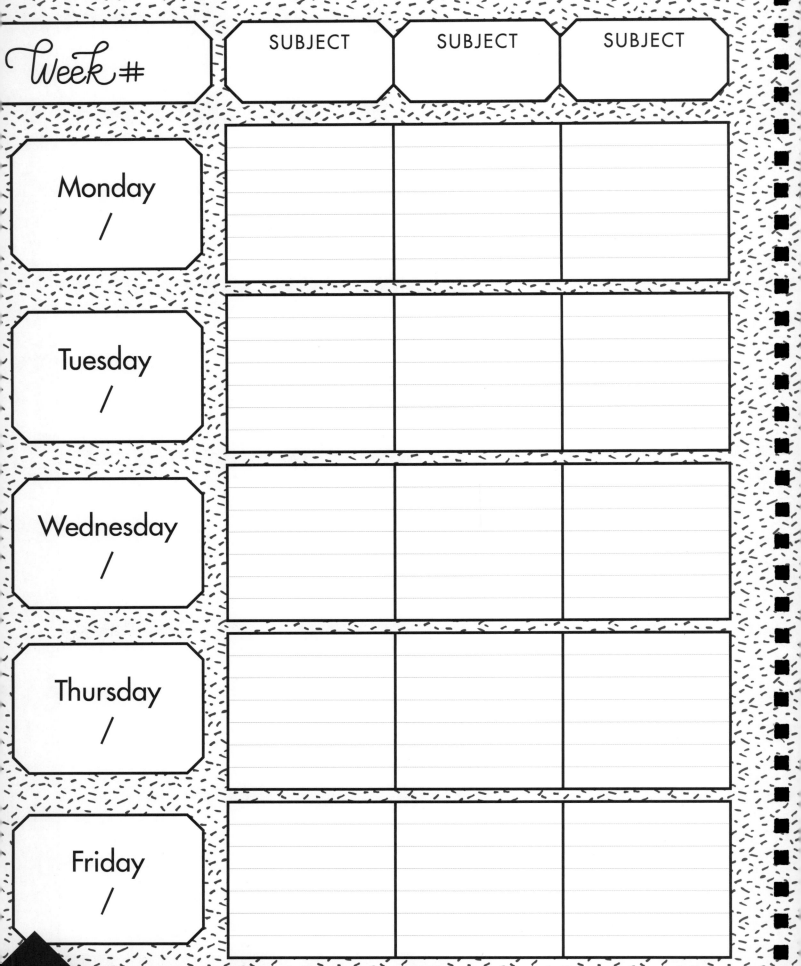

Week #

SUBJECT	SUBJECT	SUBJECT

Monday
/

Tuesday
/

Wednesday
/

Thursday
/

Friday
/

SUBJECT	SUBJECT	SUBJECT

SUBJECT	SUBJECT	SUBJECT	SUBJECT

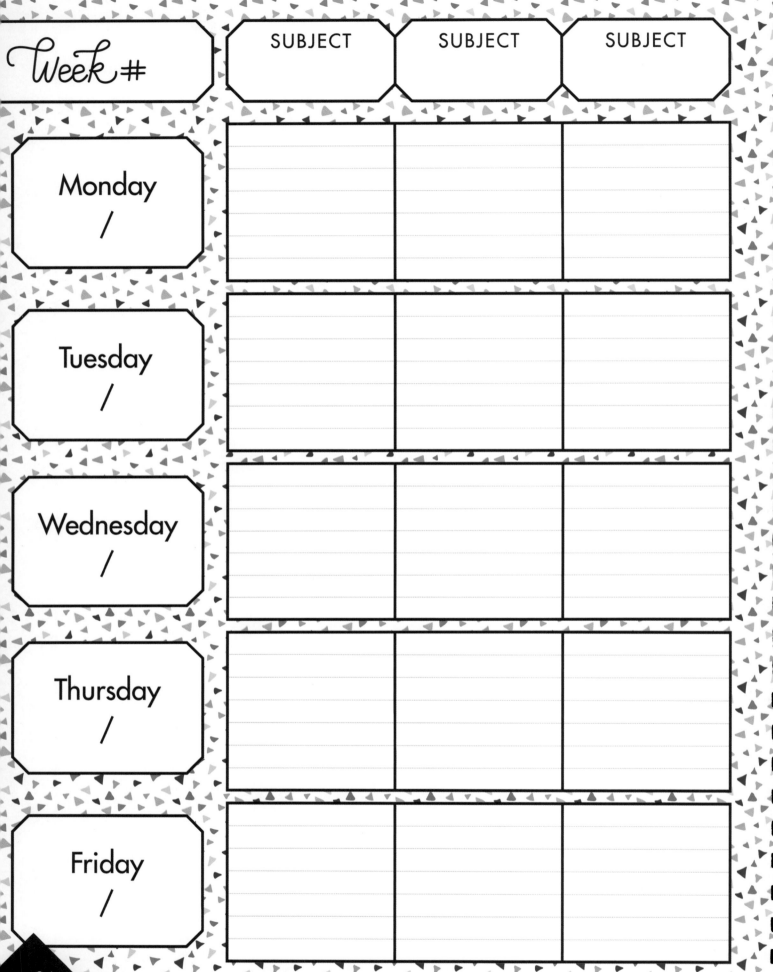

Week #

	SUBJECT	SUBJECT	SUBJECT
Monday /			
Tuesday /			
Wednesday /			
Thursday /			
Friday /	SUBJECT	SUBJECT	SUBJECT

SUBJECT	SUBJECT	SUBJECT	SUBJECT

Week

	SUBJECT	SUBJECT	SUBJECT
Monday /			
Tuesday /			
Wednesday /			
Thursday /			
Friday /			

	SUBJECT	SUBJECT	SUBJECT

Week #

	SUBJECT	SUBJECT	SUBJECT
Monday /			
Tuesday /			
Wednesday /			
Thursday /			
Friday /			

SUBJECT	SUBJECT	SUBJECT	SUBJECT

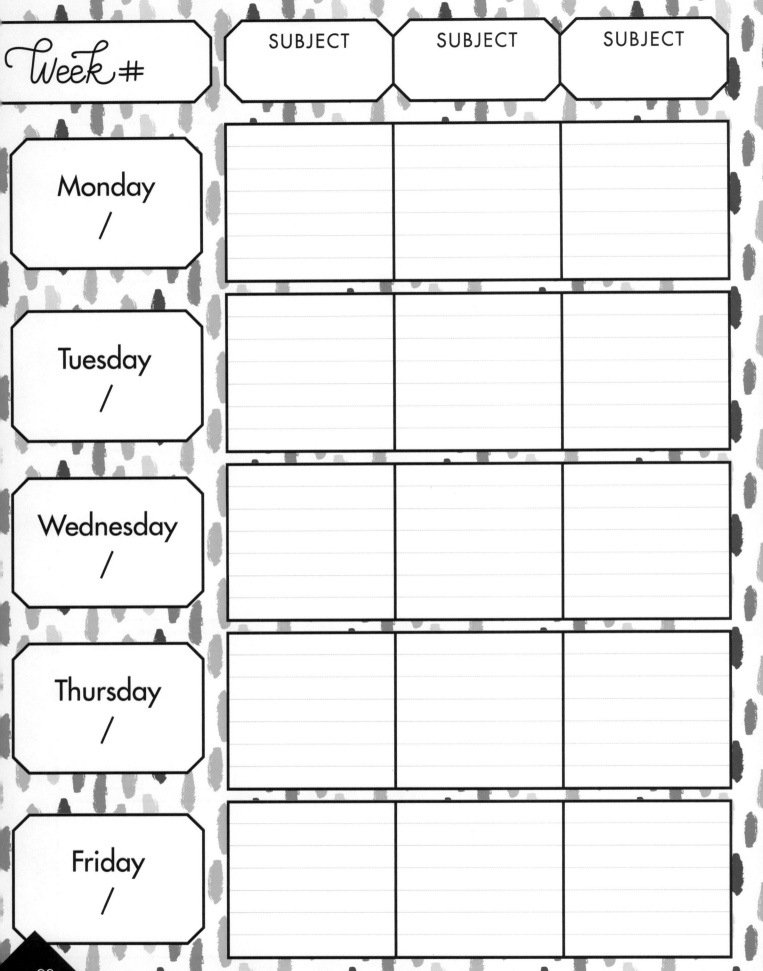

Week #

SUBJECT	SUBJECT	SUBJECT

Monday
/

Tuesday
/

Wednesday
/

Thursday
/

Friday
/

SUBJECT	SUBJECT	SUBJECT

SUBJECT	SUBJECT	SUBJECT	SUBJECT

Week

	SUBJECT	SUBJECT	SUBJECT
Monday /			
Tuesday /			
Wednesday /			
Thursday /			
Friday /			

	SUBJECT	SUBJECT	SUBJECT

SUBJECT	SUBJECT	SUBJECT	SUBJECT

Week

SUBJECT	SUBJECT	SUBJECT

Monday /

Tuesday /

Wednesday /

Thursday /

Friday /

SUBJECT	SUBJECT	SUBJECT	SUBJECT
SUBJECT	SUBJECT	SUBJECT	SUBJECT

Week #

SUBJECT	SUBJECT	SUBJECT

Monday /

Tuesday /

Wednesday /

Thursday /

Friday /

SUBJECT	SUBJECT	SUBJECT

SUBJECT	SUBJECT	SUBJECT	SUBJECT

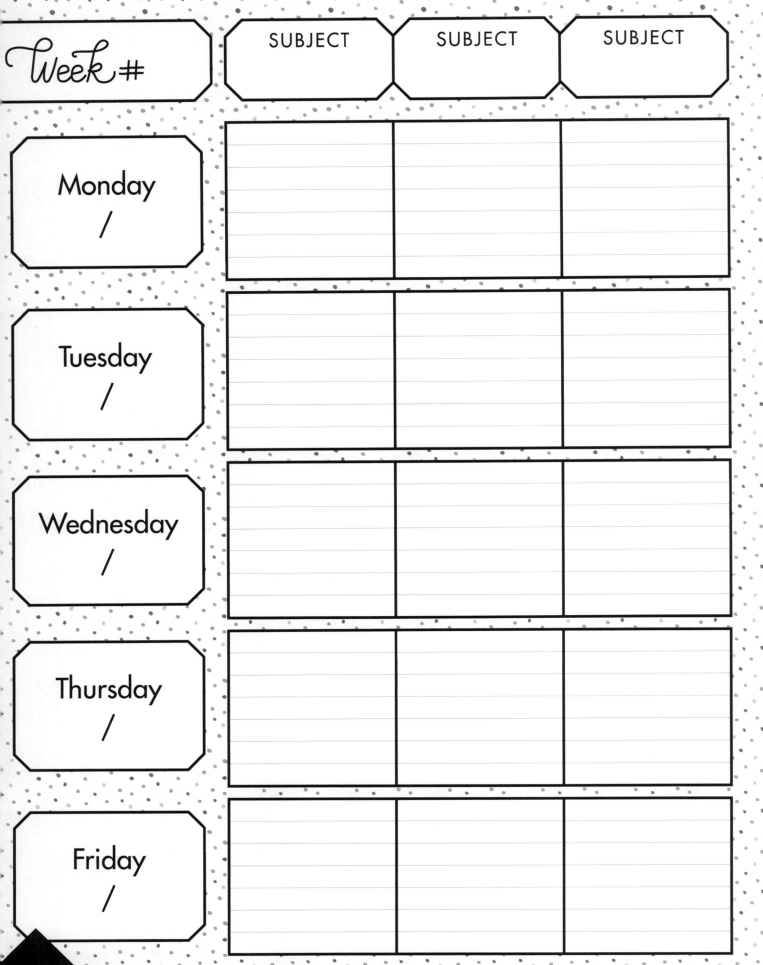

Week #

SUBJECT SUBJECT SUBJECT

Monday /

Tuesday /

Wednesday /

Thursday /

Friday /

SUBJECT SUBJECT SUBJECT

SUBJECT	SUBJECT	SUBJECT	SUBJECT

SUBJECT	SUBJECT	SUBJECT	SUBJECT

Week #

	SUBJECT	SUBJECT	SUBJECT
Monday /			
Tuesday /			
Wednesday /			
Thursday /			
Friday /			

SUBJECT	SUBJECT	SUBJECT	SUBJECT

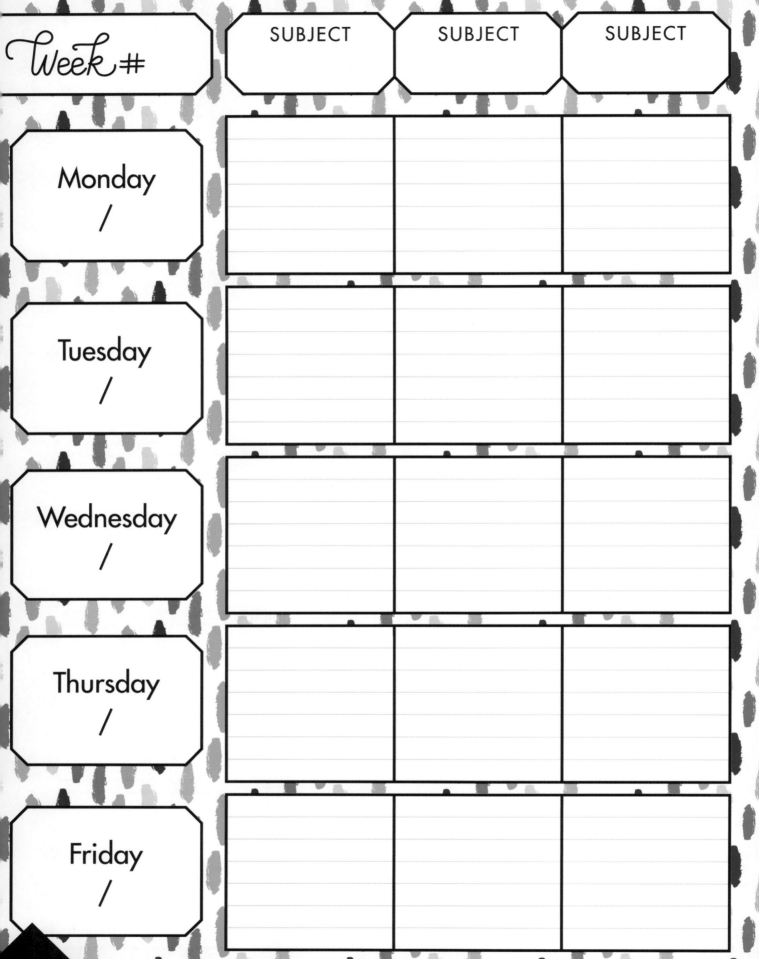

Week #

SUBJECT	SUBJECT	SUBJECT
Monday /		
Tuesday /		
Wednesday /		
Thursday /		
Friday /		

SUBJECT	SUBJECT	SUBJECT	SUBJECT

Week

	SUBJECT	SUBJECT	SUBJECT
Monday /			
Tuesday /			
Wednesday /			
Thursday /			
Friday /			

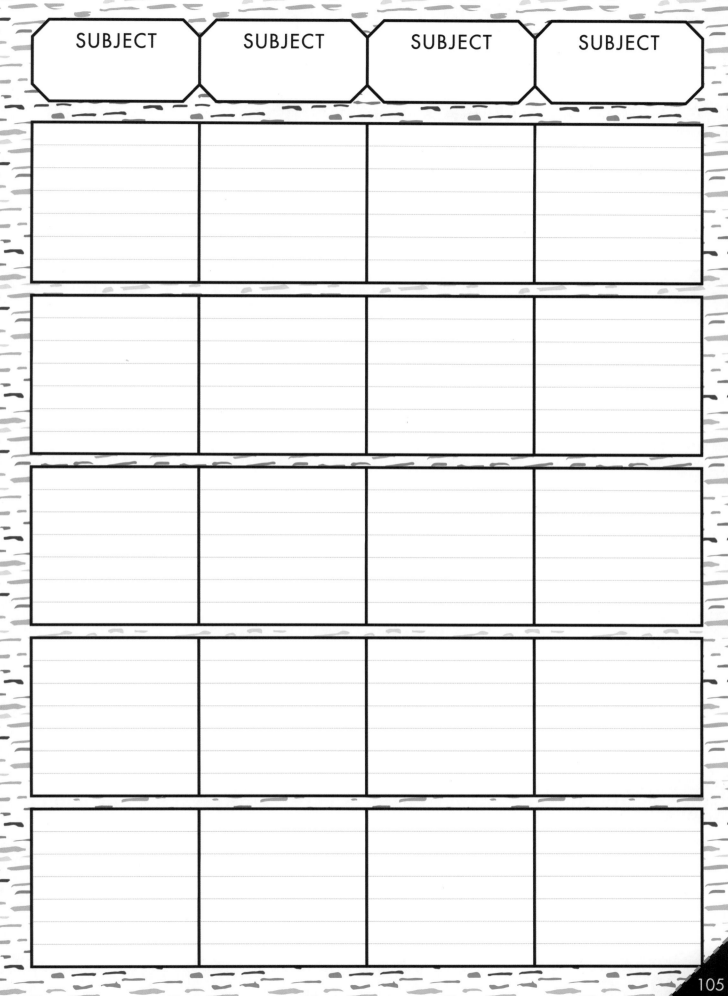

SUBJECT	SUBJECT	SUBJECT	SUBJECT

Week #

	SUBJECT	SUBJECT	SUBJECT
Monday /			
Tuesday /			
Wednesday /			
Thursday /			
Friday /			

SUBJECT	SUBJECT	SUBJECT	SUBJECT

Week

SUBJECT	SUBJECT	SUBJECT

Monday
/

Tuesday
/

Wednesday
/

Thursday
/

Friday
/

SUBJECT	SUBJECT	SUBJECT	SUBJECT

SUBJECT	SUBJECT	SUBJECT	SUBJECT

Week

	SUBJECT	SUBJECT	SUBJECT
Monday /			
Tuesday /			
Wednesday /			
Thursday /			
Friday /			
	SUBJECT	SUBJECT	SUBJECT

SUBJECT	SUBJECT	SUBJECT	SUBJECT

Week

	SUBJECT	SUBJECT	SUBJECT
Monday /			
Tuesday /			
Wednesday /			
Thursday /			
Friday /			

	SUBJECT	SUBJECT	SUBJECT

SUBJECT	SUBJECT	SUBJECT	SUBJECT

SUBJECT SUBJECT SUBJECT SUBJECT

SUBJECT	SUBJECT	SUBJECT

Monday /

Tuesday /

Wednesday /

Thursday /

Friday /

SUBJECT	SUBJECT	SUBJECT

CHECKLIST

Name

CHECKLIST

Name

PSST! CUT THIS SECTION OFF SO YOU ONLY HAVE TO WRITE YOUR CLASS LIST ONCE.

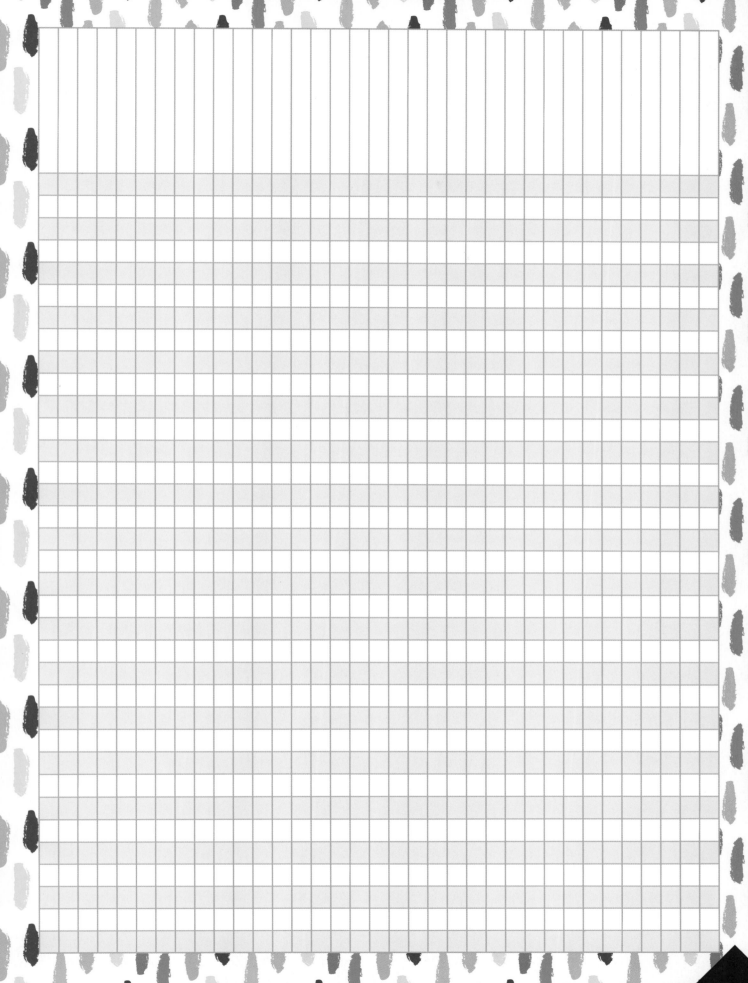

CHECKLIST

Name

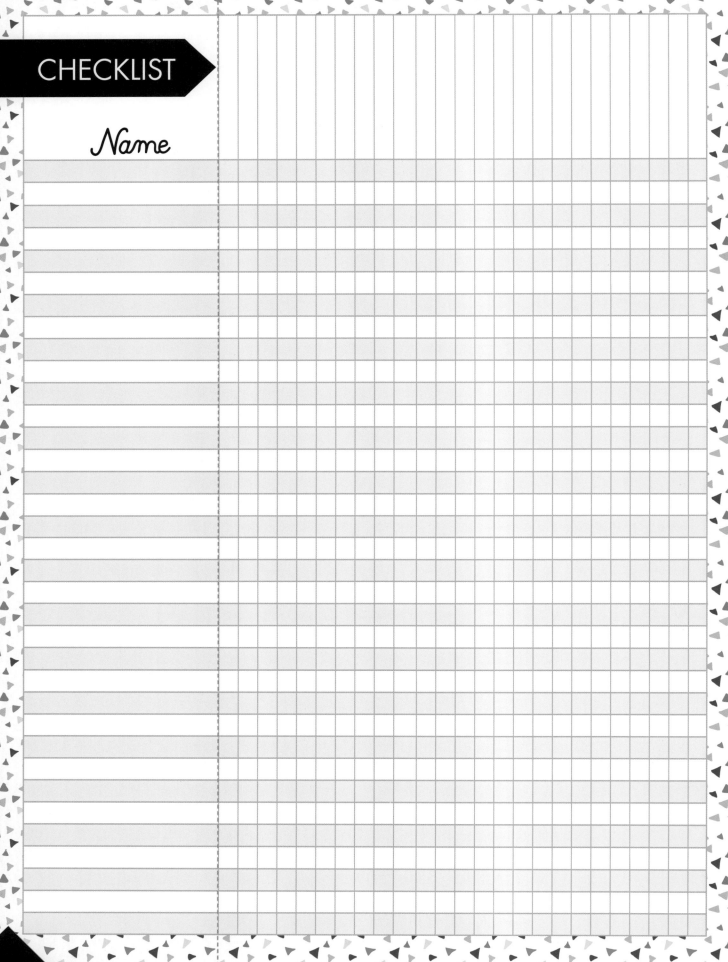

CHECKLIST

Name

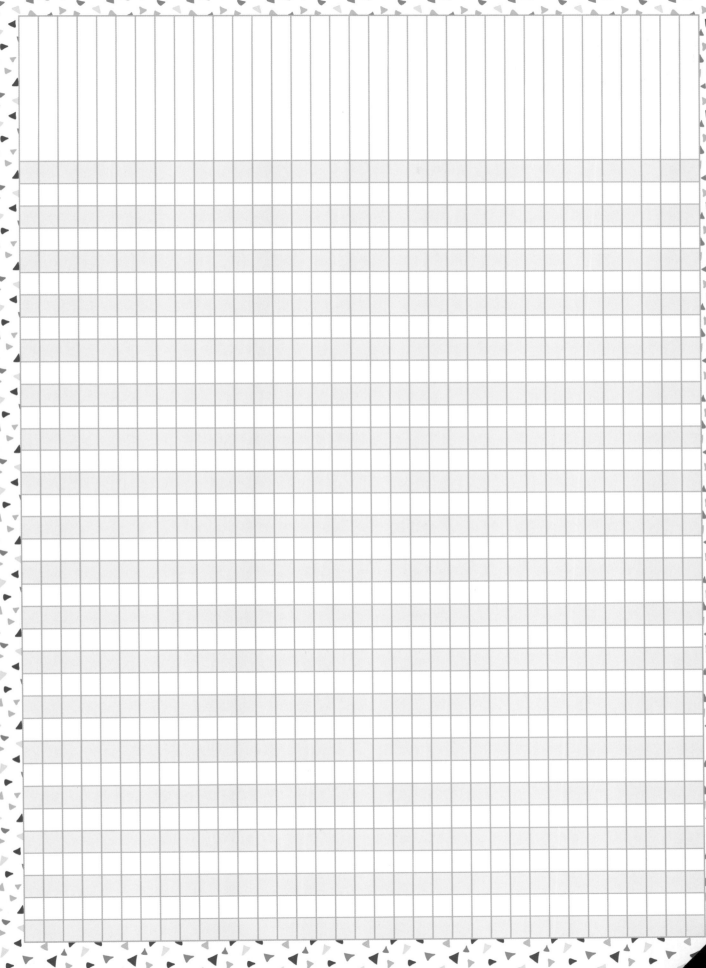

CHECKLIST

Name

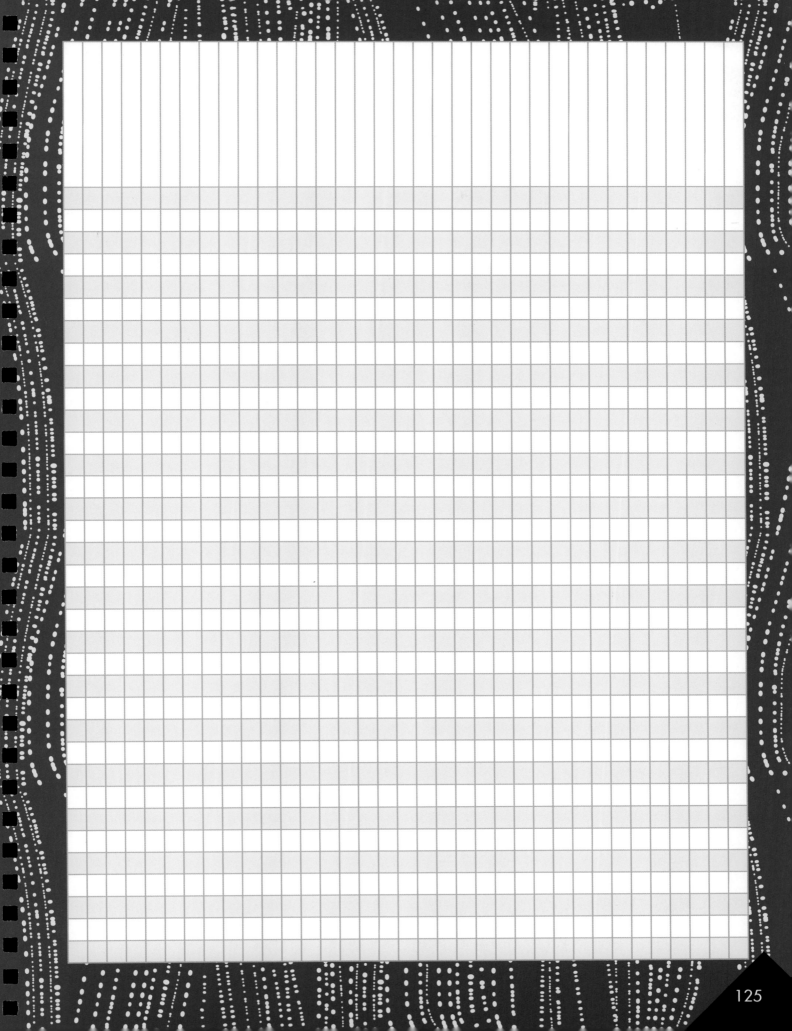

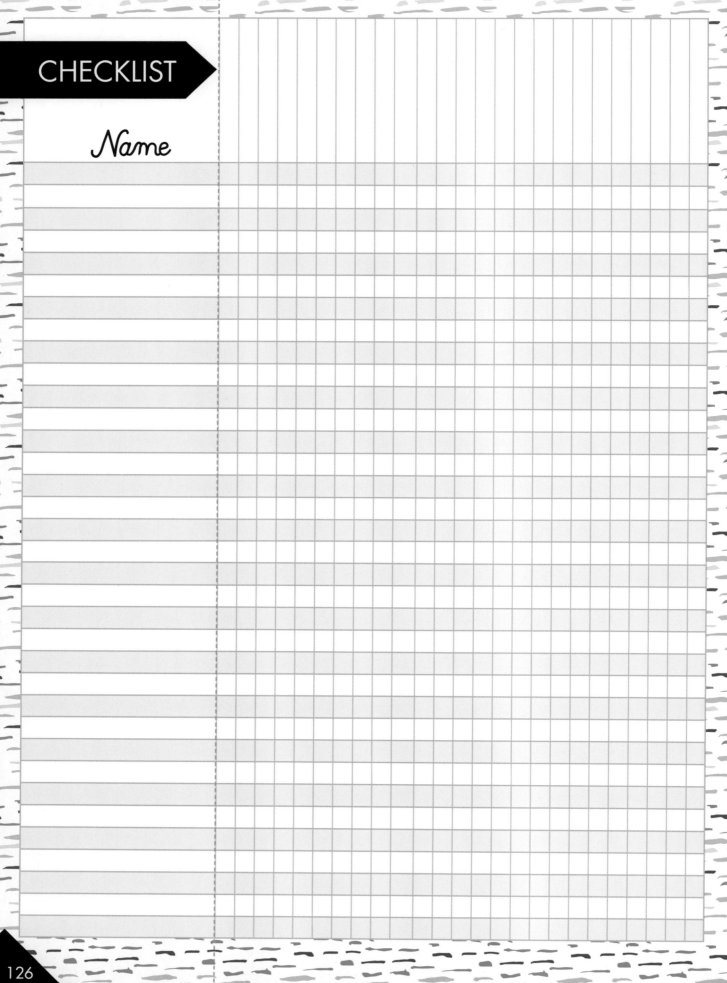

CHECKLIST

Name

RADIATE Positivity

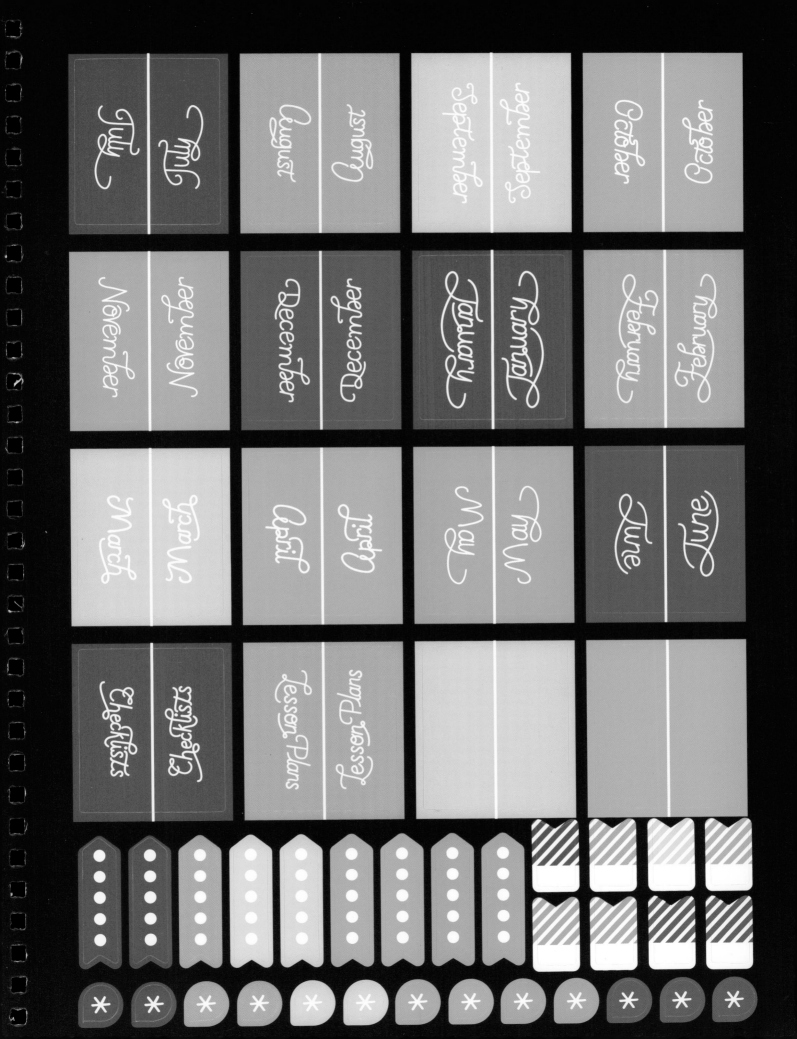